THE TELESALES POCKETBOOK

By Peter Wyllie

Drawings by Phil Hailstone

Published by:
Management Pocketbooks Ltd
Laurel House, Station Approach, Alresford, Hants SO24 9JH, U.K.
Tel: +44 (0)1962 735573 Fax: +44 (0)1962 733637
E-mail: sales@pocketbook.co.uk
Website: www.pocketbook.co.uk

First published 1996. Reprinted 1998, 2000, 2003, 2006.

© 1996 Peter Wyllie

ISBN-13   978 1 870471 39 8
ISBN-10   1 870471 39 3

British Library Cataloguing-in-Publication Data – A catalogue record for this book is available from the British Library.

Design, typesetting and graphics by **efex ltd**.   Printed in U.K.

CONTENTS

KNOWING & DOING

This book does not contain ideas that seem OK in theory but which don't work in practice. It is packed with **proven, workable** ideas based on the experience of successful telephone salespeople across a wide range of companies and industries.

As you read the ideas in this book, ask yourself two questions:

1) **'Do I know this?'** - if the answer is 'No', then work out how to use the idea in your business and your job. If the answer is 'Yes, I do know that', then ask the second question.

2) **'Do I do it - and do I do it all the time?'** - in selling, you don't get paid for what you know, only for what you do!

INTRODUCTION

PROS AND CONS

Why use the phone?

- Cost effective compared to field sales
- Immediate - often no appointment is needed
- It is personal - we can show our personality
- It is less formal than writing
- Everyone uses the phone!

Dangers of using the phone

- Slapdash approach - not prepared
- Over confidence - seeming 'pushy'
- Bad habits - developed from personal phone use
- 'Intimate zone' contact - too loud!
- It is a window on our company - what do callers see through it?

BACK TO BASICS

BACK TO BASICS

WHY THE BASICS?

For experienced salespeople

- A refresher/reminder - we forget them!

- Revisiting what we know
    - they make more sense with experience
    - they get us back on track

For new salespeople

- They are a solid foundation on which to build

- The keys to unlock the door to success

(4)

BACK TO BASICS

1. CHECK YOUR ATTITUDE

Enjoy selling

Two people can work for the same company, selling the same products to the same market place; one is an outstanding success, the other barely scrapes by.

Why?

It is often down to how much they enjoy the job!

Do we like to deal with miseries ... **NO!**
Neither do our customers.

We all have days that we would rather
forget, but we still have to present
a cheerful face to our customers -
day in and day out.

How can it be done?

1. CHECK YOUR ATTITUDE

Enjoy selling

- **Recognise the importance of selling**

    - it is vital to your company's success
    - it provides wealth
    - production without sales is scrap!
    - don't be arrogant - just confident

- **Dress for success**

    - you can't be seen, but it is still vital
    - when you look good - you feel good
    - dress for yourself, not the customers

1. CHECK YOUR ATTITUDE

Become customer focused

- **Go the extra mile - surprise your customers -** treat them as you would like to be treated

  - do more than they expect
  - address them by name
  - keep records about them
  - keep promises - or keep them informed

- **'Own the problem' -** take responsibility for dealing with complaints

  - follow up until resolved
  - don't pass the buck

1. CHECK YOUR ATTITUDE

Be enthusiastic

Definition: **Selling is transferred enthusiasm**

Nobody wants to deal with a 'misery' on the phone - remember that the phone dilutes and diffuses, so you often have to work hard to avoid sounding 'down in the dumps'.

There is only one thing that is more contagious than enthusiasm, and that is the lack of it!

- **Smile**
    - it is the shortest distance between two people
    - it is a little curve that puts everything straight
    - you reap what you sow; when you are cheerful it makes the other person respond more positively

- **Try the 'Glum' test**
    - pull a long face - look really miserable, then say 'hello, it's good to talk to you' - convinced?
    - now smile - go on, really wrinkle up, and say the same words - better, isn't it?

2. CHECK YOUR DRIVE

Set goals for personal achievement

- Don't just use the company target
  - number of calls you can make
  - number of appointments/sales you achieve
  - % above target or % improvement
- Challenge others in the team to a contest
- Reward yourself for achievement - treat yourself to a gift for reaching your goal

Get going early in the day

- Get some success to start the day
- Success breeds success
- Avoid the 'drift start'
- Plan the night before
- Have a positive expectation

3. CHECK YOUR CONFIDENCE

Have TOTAL belief in your products/services

If you don't believe in your products or services, how can you expect the customers to believe in them?

- Uncertainty breeds uncertainty
- Knowledge brings confidence
- Think of the value to the customer
- Ask for letters of reference to boost your confidence and to use with prospects

You have to pass the Mirror Test:

Look yourself in the eye and say *'If I was in the market to buy the type of product or service that I sell, I would buy my product, from my company, at the price my company charges because we are the best and offer the greatest value for money'*.

Do you really believe this? When the answer is 'Yes', then you have total belief.

3. CHECK YOUR CONFIDENCE

Stand up to make or take important calls

Standing up will make you more lively and enthusiastic.
You can be more expressive, assertive and positive
- you will sound more confident.

- The brain thinks up to 3 times faster when you are standing up

- You can be more forceful

- You will feel more alert

- It stops interruptions from other people, because they can see that you are making an important call

(11)

4. CHECK YOUR LISTENING SKILLS

Don't be a 'motor-mouth'!

There are some salespeople who believe that you should 'hit the phone with your mouth running'. Not so!

The greatest myth in selling

There is a myth in selling that salespeople must have the gift of the gab - this is not true.

Do we recognise the glib, slick, fast talking salesperson? ... YES!
Do we like them? ... NO!
Do we trust them? ... NO!
Do we buy from them? ... NO!

They are recognised, disliked and generally not trusted - **it is bad selling**.

It has been said 'When God created man he was fully equipped for selling and given **two ears** and **one mouth**'. We should use them in at least that proportion.

4. CHECK YOUR LISTENING SKILLS

Why should we listen?

- You need to find out about your customer   - you can't sell until you know
                               - you can't know until you listen
- There is no greater compliment you can pay another person than to listen to their views and opinions
- You will pick up clues about what they want that will help you to sell to them
- People talking about themselves lose track of time; a call will be more productive

How should we listen?

- Avoid interrupting
- Listen out loud!   - *Yes, I see - Oh, really? - Uh uh -*
                      - Ask little 'prod' questions
                      - Repeat back their words as a question *'You don't like them?'*
- Listen to good radio presenters interviewing; how do they demonstrate to their listeners that they are listening?

5. DEVELOP YOUR VERBAL & VOCAL SKILLS

The telephone is non-visual

In normal face to face dialogue, research
has shown that communication is:

7%   the words we say

38%   the way we say them

55%   non verbal signals

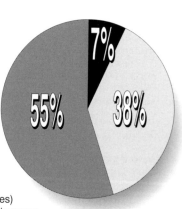

Clearly you can only use the first two when
you are on the phone (until the age of video phones)
so you are potentially only operating at 45% effectiveness;
unless you compensate by making more use of the other two.

5. DEVELOP YOUR VERBAL & VOCAL SKILLS

They can't see you - you can't see them

- You can't **show** them products or literature
- They can't **see** that you are sincere
- You can't **see** their reactions

But you still have to:

- Present your ideas to them
- Get their feedback
- Know how it's going
- Know when to move on
- Know when to ask for the order

5. DEVELOP YOUR VERBAL & VOCAL SKILLS

Focus on the voice

- Be warm and sincere
- Use the voice to build trust
- Don't speak too quickly

- Don't mumble
- Don't SHOUT
- Lower the voice for maturity
  - avoid squeaking

Paint word pictures

'Imagine' is a command to the brain that it has to obey!

Read this: *Imagine that you are walking on a sandy beach beneath a clear blue sky, with palm trees gently swaying in the breeze.* What did you see?

You read words, yet saw pictures! Try to paint pictures with the words that you use on the telephone:

- How good they will feel about their decision
- Pride of ownership
- Peace of mind

- Enhanced productivity
- Happier staff
- Less aggravation

BACK TO BASICS

5. DEVELOP YOUR VERBAL & VOCAL SKILLS

Avoid negative language

- **Possibly - maybe - perhaps**
- We **might** be able to do this
- I **hope** that will be OK
- **If** you decide to buy it ...

Use positive language

- I am **sure** that will do the job
- I **know** we can get that for you
- I'm **certain** you'll be pleased with this
- **Once** you've taken delivery

5. DEVELOP YOUR VERBAL & VOCAL SKILLS

Ask questions to keep control and get feedback

When you are asked a question, try to answer it with a question - to keep control of the conversation, eg:

'How soon can you deliver?' - **'How soon do you need them?'**
'What is your best price?' - **'What volume are you wanting?'**
'Do you make a larger version?' - **'What size did you need?'**

Sometimes you have to give information. On those occasions you should use the 'statement/question' **(S/Q)** technique, eg:

'I can get it to you by Thursday' (S) - **'Would that be soon enough?' (Q)**
'I've only got one left in that size' (S) - **'Shall I reserve it for you?' (Q)**

5. DEVELOP YOUR VERBAL & VOCAL SKILLS

Ask commitment gaining questions

- *'Is that the kind of thing you are looking for?'*
- *'How soon can I expect your order?'*
- *'Can you fax me the confirmation today?'*

Use 'Tie-down' questions

Tie-downs are little phrases that are added on to statements to get agreement. For example, 'Isn't it?', 'Wouldn't you?', 'Won't you?', 'Doesn't it?', etc.

By using these, you can get agreement from a prospect for statements that you have made. It is as powerful as the person making the statement themselves, eg:

- *'That's a good price - **isn't it?'***
- *'You really want the best value for money - **don't you?'***
- *'That should be perfect for you - **shouldn't it?'***
- *"You don't want to spend more than you have to - **do you?'***

6. CHECK YOUR PREPARATION

Be prepared for questions you may be asked.

Know your products

- Get to know all the products (if you sell a vast range, know where to find the information)
- Know the features, the advantages over other products and the potential benefits to the customer
- Know what makes them superior and how to justify the price

Know your company/your suppliers' companies

- Its track record
- Company procedures and policies
- Delivery times
- Pricing
- Terms of business
- Where to go for help!

6. CHECK YOUR PREPARATION

Be prepared for the day's work

What do you need to have ready to take or make calls, fix appointments, give quotations and take orders?

- Company and product literature
- Price lists
- Order forms
- Route map for journey/delivery planning
- Diary
- Call logging sheets

- Record cards
- Notepads
- Pens

Remember the 7 Ps:

PERFORMANCE

POOR

PATHETICALLY

PREVENTS

PLANNING

PRIOR

PROPER

7. CHECK YOUR CALL HANDLING TECHNIQUE

Introduction

Four types of in-coming call

1 Orders
2 Enquiries about products/services
3 General queries about orders/accounts, etc
4 Complaints

In this section we will look at the techniques for handling in-coming calls that apply to all of the above types.

BACK TO BASICS

7. CHECK YOUR CALL HANDLING TECHNIQUE

First impressions last!

Answering the phone correctly is vital.

When you answer the phone, you don't know:
- Who is calling
- Where they are from
- What they want

- Whether they have ever called your company before
- What mood they are in

It could be that they:
- Are wanting to place the biggest order in your company's history
- Have just been let down by your major competitor
- Are giving you your last chance to put something right before they go to one of your competitors
- Have just seen an advertisement, and know nothing else about you

Whatever the reason - **you will never get a second chance to make a positive first impression!**

(23)

7. CHECK YOUR CALL HANDLING TECHNIQUE

First impressions last!

You will make an impression of some kind! What will it be?

- Harassed, busy and 'Let's get it over'
- Distant, cold, uninterested
- Warm and friendly
- Professional and helpful

The telephone is the window through which customers see your company. Will what they see entice them, or put them off?

Answer the phone in 2 - 3 rings

- Answer on the first ring and they will be taken by surprise and may not be ready; or they will think that you've nothing else to do!
- More than 3 - 4 rings and they may think that you don't care or that you are too busy already!

Getting it right is vital

How do you feel when you call a company and the phone just rings and rings and nobody answers? That is how your callers will feel if you don't answer the phone.

24

7. CHECK YOUR CALL HANDLING TECHNIQUE

Use the correct sequence

For Reception/switchboard - cheerful greeting
1   Greeting - *'Good morning'/'Good afternoon'*   2   Company name

This is acceptable for a switchboard, because people are expecting to be put through to another person or department.

Within your department (or if everyone answers outside calls)

1	Greeting (*'Good morning'*)	- they have a chance to 'tune in' to your voice
2	Company/dept name (*'Sales office'*)	- they know they've got the right place!
3	Your name (*'you're speaking to Alan'*)	- people deal with people, not companies
4	Ask a question (*'What can we do for you?'*)	- it gets them talking
		- you then know how to help them

Big danger! - too often people recite this like a mindless answering machine. Use your personality and vary the phrases you say so you don't get bored.

Done badly it's a turn-off - **so do it well!**

(25)

7. CHECK YOUR CALL HANDLING TECHNIQUE

Find out who's calling - ASK - SPELL - REPEAT

1 Ask their name - *'May I ask your name, please?'* - *'And your name is?'*
2 Check the spelling
   - how do you feel when people write to you and get your name wrong?
   - their name will be appearing on letters, quotes, proposals, orders, delivery notes and invoices; get the name wrong, and you may not get as far as the last three items!
3 Write it down for accuracy
4 Check the pronunciation
   - if you are going to use their name, then you need to get it right to avoid annoying them (they will correct you early on without embarrassment)
5 Use their name in the conversation
   - it is the sweetest sound in the world to them
   - you are building rapport
   - it is part of the 'massaging' process

7. CHECK YOUR CALL HANDLING TECHNIQUE

Don't let customers overhear what they shouldn't

If there is a need to speak to a colleague, use the 'secrecy' button or the 'mute' key rather than just putting a hand over the phone. It can create the wrong impression if customers hear:

- *'That last lot were all damaged, weren't they?'*
- *'I've got some wally on the phone ...'*
- *'Didn't you have one that fell apart last week?'*
- *'Those idiots in despatch have got another one wrong.'*
- *'Can you have a word with him, he doesn't believe me.'*

Don't leave callers on hold

If you have to put someone on hold while they are waiting to be connected, you should aim to speak to them about every 20-30 seconds to let them know that they haven't been lost in the system, and to give them the opportunity to leave their number or to call back.

27

7. CHECK YOUR CALL HANDLING TECHNIQUE

End the call professionally

You will have developed a rapport with a caller in a brief space of time - how you end the call can either reinforce or destroy that rapport.

Seven steps to end a call professionally:

1   Confirm back the agreed details - in detail
2   Thank them - for their call/order/enquiry, etc
3   Ask for help (if appropriate) - best time to call them next, how to find them, etc
4   Look forward to the next contact
5   Leave on a pleasant note - *'Have a good weekend'* (note: avoid 'Have a nice day'!)
6   Say goodbye
7   **Put the phone down - LAST**
    Wait for the 'click' at their end. This important step is missed by most people
    using the telephone: - it avoids a 'cut-off' feeling
                       - they may remember something else they wish to say

BACK TO BASICS

8. CHECK YOUR COMPLAINT HANDLING TECHNIQUE

Turn complaints into opportunities

Every company gets complaints - if they get none at all, then they are either perfect (unlikely) or they just don't do enough business! Popular theory was that customers whose complaints were satisfactorily resolved would still not be as happy as they had been before they complained. **Not true!** Experience shows that, if a complaint is handled well, customers will be **more satisfied afterwards.**

How to handle complaints

1 Listen! - allow them to let off steam; don't interrupt; note all relevant details
2 Question for more information and clarification
3 Summarise back and gain agreement
4 Thank them for drawing it to your attention; it diffuses the situation
5 Promise action and a call back to advise
6 Look into the situation and get all the facts
7 Call the customer back - keep the promise even if you have nothing to report
8 Tell the customer what will be done to put things right
9 Keep in touch until the matter is resolved - let them know of progress/delays
10 Call them after resolution to reinforce

9. DO IT NOW!

Procrastination is my sin
It brings me endless sorrow
I really ought to pack it in
I will! I'll start tomorrow.

After each call:

1   Update records while it is fresh in the memory
    - ready for the next contact
    - 'the faintest of ink lasts longer than the sharpest of memory'
2   Process paperwork - orders/quotes
    - nothing gets lost
    - it avoids build-up and end of day rush
3   Diarise the next contact to ensure prompt follow-up
4   Make the next call

Tips to improve work flow

- If sending out literature, etc, address the envelope; list what is to be included on a Post-it note, then fill the envelopes during your next break
- Do the same for letters confirming appointment
- Have set times for letter writing
- Keep separate trays for orders, quotes and letters

MAKING THE SALE

THE PSYCHOLOGY OF A SALE

Selling is very simple; it can be summarised as four distinct steps:

1   Get a person's attention/arouse curiosity
2   Establish/find out what they want
3   Show them how you can give them what they want
4   Ask for a commitment

What are the steps to achieve the result you need?

> **A** roused curiosity/attention
> **I** nterest in doing something
> **D** esire for one product specifically
> **A** ction

These four stages represent selling at its simplest. Selling is simple - it's not **easy**, but it is simple! Each step leads naturally to the next, and the customer will go with you if you take it one step at a time. If you try to jump a step, it may be too big a jump for the customer.

THE PSYCHOLOGY OF A SALE

BUILDING DESIRE

The aim is that, over the period of the sales call, you build interest and desire in your customer to the point where, if you ask for a commitment, they will answer positively.

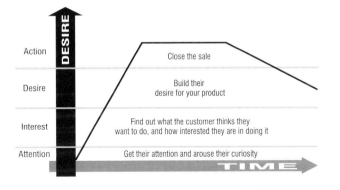

Action — Close the sale

Desire — Build their desire for your product

Interest — Find out what the customer thinks they want to do, and how interested they are in doing it

Attention — Get their attention and arouse their curiosity

If no commitment is given and time passes by with no action or commitment, then desire can fall and the sale be lost.

(33)

THE FOUR STEPS

1. Attention - arouse curiosity

- With an **in-coming** call, this has already been achieved by advertising, marketing & PR, mailshots, a referral, etc

- When you make **out-going** calls, then you have to get the prospect's attention and arouse their curiosity yourself; this can be done by:
  - using relevant suggested benefit statements
  - asking pertinent, problem-related questions

2. Establish the level of interest in doing something, and raise it

- There are four steps in this process:
  1 **Probe** to find out what they want
  2 **Introduce** things that they may not have thought of
  3 **Summarise or prioritise**
  4 **Pre-close** to test their commitment to purchasing

We call this the question funnel.

THE FOUR STEPS

3. Convert their interest in doing something into desire for your product

- Show them how you can do what they want
- Match what you offer to their requirements
- Explain the benefits relevant to them
- Answer any questions
- Check that they are happy with your offering

4. Action - ask for commitment

- Get feedback throughout the presentation
- Handle all concerns and resistance as they arise
- Use frequent trial closes
- Ask for a commitment!

THE QUESTION FUNNEL

OPEN QUESTIONS
to gain information

CLOSED QUESTIONS
to gain confirmation

CLOSED QUESTIONS
for commitment
and to
prioritize

Suggestions
are added to widen
the prospect's horizons

Pre Close on the objective

MAKING THE SALE

IN-COMING CALLS

RULES FOR TAKING ORDERS

Rule 1 - Take the order!
- Their company details
- Correct delivery/invoice addresses
- Product details and quantities

Rule 2 - Check it is what the customer wants
- If the wrong items are delivered, they will blame you
- Check what it is to be used for

Rule 3 - Sell up and across the product range
If all you do is to take their order, you could be replaced with an answering machine.

- Use link phrases:
  - *'Did you realise that we also offer ...'*
  - *'Were you aware that we also have ...'*
  - *'Many of our customers now order ...'*
  - *'Have you heard about the new ...'*

- Ask about ancillary products
- Explain about special promotions

Rule 4 - Confirm the order back, in detail
Rule 5 - Use the correct call-ending sequence (see Basic 7)

MAKING THE SALE

IN-COMING ORDERS
ADDITIONAL CHECKS

Credit status
- Do they have an account?
- Are they on hold?
- Should you ask for payment before processing?
- Is this 'payment with order'?

Authorisation
- Is an official order needed?
- Will they send confirmation?
- Is the order provisional until then?

New customers
- Where did they hear of you?
- What prompted them to call?
- Who have they been using?
- What else do they buy?

OUT-GOING CALLS

What makes you think out-going calls are harder?

With in-coming calls you have no control over:

- Who you talk to
- When you talk to them
- What they want to talk about

You can only be **reactive** not **proactive!**

On out-going calls you can control:

- Who you call
- When you call
- What you call about

**But many salespeople still
find it difficult. Why?**

OUT-GOING CALLS

Why?

It is the basic fear of one little word ...

NO!

If a company has not heard of you, or seen your marketing, and you never call them - what is the answer you have got in any case? **NO!**

But you have forced the 'no' on them.

If you call them and get a 'no', you are no worse off than you were. If, on the other hand, you call them and get a 'yes', then you are better off. **Either way you win!**

OUT-GOING CALLS

Remember: SW, SW, SW, SW, N

No, not compass directions but:

SOME WILL

SOME WON'T

SO WHAT?

SHAN'T WORRY

NEXT!

The key to confidence is
PLANNING and **PREPARATION**.

MAKING THE SALE

PLANNING CALLS

Plan for achievement

- **Set goals and targets**
  - number/value of sales
  - number of quotations
  - number of decision-maker contacts

- **Know your personal ratio averages**
  - calls: decision-maker contact
  - decision-maker contact: quotations
  - quotations: order
  - average order value

- **Plan blocks of time for calling**
  - break goals into smaller chunks
  - pre-determine breaks
  - set mini-targets
  - long enough for productive calling
  - short enough to see the end
  - small steps lead to great strides

MAKING THE SALE

THE NEED FOR TARGETS

- **Goals and targets**
    - give focus to work
    - motivate to succeed
    - enable you to measure progress

- **Personal averages**
    - give you a yardstick to work by
    - motivate you to continue when times are hard
    - show you where improvements are needed

- **Time allocation**
    - you can 'get in the swing' without interruption
    - leaves room for admin between blocks
    - middle distance not marathon!

PLAN THE CALL CAMPAIGN

- **Who shall I target?**
  - companies in the same field
  - a specific geographic area
  - section(s) of my card file/database
  - section(s) of a directory

- **Print or prepare a list**
  - it removes 'Who do I call next?'
  - easier to monitor progress
  - research shows up to **3 times as many calls** when salespeople use a list

PLAN THE CALL CAMPAIGN

- **Research the companies**

  - aim high when you call; it is easier to be passed down from on high than referred up from below!

  - try phoning the M.D.'s secretary? **Tip:** The M.D.'s secretary can be a fount of knowledge and very helpful in pointing you in the right direction.

  - key question: *'I wonder if you can help me?'* invariably gets *'I will if I can!'*

  - find out what the company does

  - find out turnover/size/number of staff

MAKING THE SALE

PLAN EACH CALL

- **Who to ask for**
  - their full name and position

- **Why you are calling**
  - the reason you will give them

- **What is your objective**
  - main objective (eg: a sale)
  - the minimum you want from the call
  - fallback objectives (eg: an appointment)

- **What is your key message**
  - if you were in their position, what would interest you about your product or service?

- **How are you going to open the call**
  - what can you say to get their attention/arouse curiosity?

- **Likely obstacles and how to counter them**
  - gatekeepers and barriers (Sales Prevention Officers)
  - resistance from the decision maker

DEALING WITH RECEPTION

- **Their job is to connect calls, not necessarily to filter, so:**
  - ask to be put through to the person you want:
    'Jim Smith, please. Thank you.' - or: *'Can you put me through to Jim Smith - thank you'*
  - the 'please' is friendly; the 'thank you' denotes finality

- **If they ask 'Who shall I say is calling?'**
  - *'Sally Allen, thank you'*

- **Beware the trap question: 'What's it concerning?'**
  - don't go into a long explanation; don't try to sell
    'It's about the supplies your company purchases; he is still responsible for that, isn't he?'
  - don't say 'It's a private matter'; it can create an unnecessary barrier when he finds it isn't

DEALING WITH 'GATEKEEPERS'

- Treat them like people, not inferior objects

- Use: *'I wonder if you can help me?'*

- By-pass; call outside office hours

- Don't leave name and number for call back
  - they rarely do
  - they prejudge the reason for the call
  - if they call back, you are not prepared

MAKING THE SALE

THROUGH TO THE DECISION-MAKER

'I don't know who you are, I've never heard of your company. I'm not interested in buying anything at the moment, I'm very busy and you've caught me at a bad time. Now, what did you want to sell me?'

- Check you've got the right person - *'Is that Jim Smith, the production director?'*
- Greeting and introduce yourself and where you're from
  - *'Good afternoon, Mr Smith, my name is Sally Allen and I'm calling from ABC Ltd'*

- Give a one line description of your company - **relevant** to the **reason for the call**
  - *'We are specialists in component protection technology'*

- Give the reason for the call
  - *'The reason for my call is that I noticed you have recently won a large contract to supply specialist machined parts to the MOD'*

- Check it is convenient for them to talk
  - *'Do you have a few minutes to discuss it?'* or *'Do you have a moment?'*
    - if 'no', find out when would be convenient and arrange call back
    - any other answer, move to next step

MAKING THE SALE

THROUGH TO THE DECISION-MAKER

- Lead into an open exploratory question
  - *'We have been supplying a number of companies such as yours with a range of products to protect their components in transit; can I ask, **how** are you packaging yours at present?'*

- We now have a 'conversation with purpose', using the question funnel model - this will lead to:
  1. yes, there is an interest in what you have discussed
  2. they might be interested, but not yet
  3. they have everything well covered at the moment

- Summarise what has been discussed to lead into:
  - a sales presentation
  - agreement on some other course of action

- Present your products, relating them to their problems and explaining the benefits
- Use test closes throughout: *'How does that sound?'*
- Summarise and ask for commitment
- End of call sequence

PRESENTING ON THE TELEPHONE

- Relate product features to their problems
- Explain the benefits
- Gain agreement at each stage
- Use **'imagine'** *('imagine what a difference that will make')*
- Use only **relevant** facts/features

Matching builds desire, but effective matching builds the desire to buy from YOU.

Trial closes: these give us feedback
- *'How does that sound?'*
- *'Does that seem like the kind of thing you want?'*

Final (?) close: when all the signals are right - **ASK!**

Call ending: whatever the outcome, use the professional call ending sequence (Basic 7)

VERBAL BUYING SIGNALS

Buying signals are indicators that a customer is receptive to our ideas, and **may** be ready to commit further.

Types of buying signal

Questions
- *'What is delivery like?'*
- *'How soon can I get them?'*
- *'Can I get a sample first?'*
- *'Do you make it in red?'*

Comments
- *'That sounds better than our current method'*
- *'I saw an article about that last week which was interesting'*
- *'That's good!'*

Close on a buying signal
- *'How soon do you want them?'*
- *'Do you need them in red?'* or *'If I can get them in red, how many do you want?'*
- *'Yes, it would be a great improvement on your current method, wouldn't it?'*
- *'Yes, I saw that article, the results were impressive, weren't they? I expect you'd like those kind of returns, wouldn't you?'*

CLOSING

Closing is a process

Gaining commitment is something that must happen from the start to the finish of a call. It is the salesperson's tool for keeping the customer with them throughout. The final close is really just a confirmation of all the other closes along the way.

Keep it simple
Nothing complicated, no tricks - closing is not a con!

3 closes to use on the telephone:

1 Direct closes

These demand a 'yes' or 'no' answer.

Ask   -   the closing question
Lead   -   verbally with the answer
Listen   -   shut up! Let them answer

eg: *'So, can we go ahead on that basis, then - yes?'*
      'I'll order the red one for you then - OK?'

MAKING THE SALE

CLOSING

2 Choice closes

These take away the choice of **whether to go ahead**, and replace it with **which, when, how, etc**

-   *'Would you prefer the red or the blue?'*   -   *'Do you want one box or two?'*

3 Assumptive closes

When the discussion has been going well, why assume that the customer is going to do anything else other than order? Take control and move it forward.

-   *'Right, I'll get that in the mail to you today; if you can just give me your credit card number'*

Final word:

If you have done your job right, the final close should almost be redundant. **The best close is when the customer asks!** When that happens, some salespeople feel that they have failed because they didn't close. In fact, the opposite is true; they did so well that the customer was eager to buy and said so.

-   *'I'm sorry, you can't order yet; I've not asked you my final closing question!'*

POTENTIAL CUSTOMERS

POTENTIAL CUSTOMERS

DEALING WITH ENQUIRIES

1. Take their details

- name
- company
- position

2. Find out

- what they want
- what level of interest they have
- where they heard of you
- why they called
- where they are on the desire graph

POTENTIAL CUSTOMERS

DEALING WITH ENQUIRIES
QUALIFY: SUSPECT OR PROSPECT?

Suspects are not prospects!

Definition: A prospect is someone who is in the market to buy the type of product or service that you sell. They have the money to make the purchase, the authority to place an order and will do so within a timescale acceptable in your industry.

POTENTIAL CUSTOMERS

DEALING WITH ENQUIRIES

M A N A C T A

Money	● Do they have enough money to buy? ● Is your price right for them?	● Is there money in the budget?
Authority	● Do they authorise orders? ● What is their ordering procedure?	● Who is the decision maker?
Need	● Do you offer what they want? ● Do they have a real need?	● Do you have to introduce ideas?
Actions	● What have they bought before? ● What else have they considered?	● What have they done so far? ● Do they seem serious?
Competition	● Are you in competition? ● Is it 'external' or 'internal'?	● Is 'do nothing' an option?
Timescale	● How soon do they want it?	● Is that realistic?
Ability	● Do you have the ability to deliver?	

DEALING WITH ENQUIRIES

- **Test commitment**
  - is this serious?
  - if you can offer them what they want, will they buy it?

- **Present your offering**
  - explain what you can offer and how it will be of benefit
  - match your product to their requirement
  - the better the perceived match, the easier the sale

- **Test their desire**
  - how does that sound?
  - is that the sort of thing you want?

- **Agree action - close on next step**
  - ask for an order
  - some other commitment
  - appointment
  - send information
  - follow up call

POTENTIAL CUSTOMERS

DEALING WITH ENQUIRIES

USE THE 'QUESTION FUNNEL'

Open probes: give you information
Open probes: develop the conversation - allowing you to introduce new topics
Closed probes: confirm what you have learned and check that you understand fully
Closed probes: allow you to test the water at various stages

Imagine a call to an electrical shop:

C/M	'I'm interested in buying a washing machine'
S/P (Open P)	*'What sort are you looking for?'*
C/M	'I want one to fit in my flat'
S/P (Open P)	*'How big is the kitchen?'*
C/M	'Not very big'
S/P (Closed P)	*'So you are looking for something which is compact, is that right?*
C/M	'Yes, very much so'
S/P (Open P)	*'How many people are going to use it?'*
C/M	'Just two of us'
S/P (Open P)	*'What else have you got in the kitchen?'*
C/M	'There's a cooker, a fridge freezer and a rather old tumble drier'

DEALING WITH ENQUIRIES

USE THE 'QUESTION FUNNEL' contd

S/P (Closed P)	*'Were you thinking of changing the tumble drier as well?'*
C/M	'I'd like to, but I don't think I can afford it at the moment'
S/P (Open P)	*'How much were you wanting to spend?'*
C/M	'No more than £300'
S/P (Closed P)	*'Well, that's a good amount to spend. Can I ask you, did you know that you could get a washing machine and tumble drier combined?'*
C/M	'No, what are they?'
S/P	*'They do the job of both and take up the space of one!'*
C/M (Buy signal)	'That sounds pretty good; how much are they?'
S/P	*'Just £350 - but we have a special trade-in offer at the moment - if you trade in your old drier, we'll give you £15 for it, so it would only be £335. So, for just £35 extra you'll get a new tumble drier too. That's good value, isn't it?'* (Closing tie-down)
C/M	'It sounds pretty good; have you got one in stock that I can see?'
S/P (Closing)	*'I've only got one left in stock. I could provisionally hold it for you - how soon could you come in?'*

POTENTIAL CUSTOMERS

SOURCES FOR NEW PROSPECTS

BE CREATIVE - BE INNOVATIVE

Inside your company:

1 Past customers - inactive sales ledger accounts
2 Look at the purchase ledger - who are your suppliers?
3 Collect business cards from salespeople prospecting your company - use them to call their decision-makers
4 Get the receptionist/secretary to collect information from salespeople prospecting your company by phone

Important note: If your company expects you to canvass for business on the telephone and then has a policy of 'repelling all boarders' towards salespeople that call your company, is this really fair on you or them?

5 Old diaries - who were you speaking to last year?
6 Old record cards
7 Ask for referrals from existing customers
8 If you have field engineers, get them to ask for referrals or look for potential prospects
9 Ask all members of other departments who they know

POTENTIAL CUSTOMERS

SOURCES FOR NEW PROSPECTS

BE CREATIVE - BE INNOVATIVE

Outside your company

1. Newspapers - national and local
   - Advertisements - products or job vacancies
   - People in the news
   - News about companies; expanding, moving, winning business

2. Trade/Industry magazines
   - Where do your customers advertise? You will find their competitors there, too
   - What are your customers' trade magazines?

3. Directories
   - Trade directories
   - Business directories - Kompass, etc
   - Yellow Pages/Business Pages/Thomsons

4. Be observant when driving/walking; carry a notepad or dictation tape recorder
5. Social contacts
6. Liaise with salespeople in non-competitive industries and swap leads
7. Competitors - you may compete in some areas, but still supply them in others, eg:
   rail competes with air on travel in the UK, but rail executives still fly to the USA
   - the Atlantic tunnel isn't open yet!

POTENTIAL CUSTOMERS

USING THE PROSPECT LIST

Keep a holding file for 'suspects'
- Press cuttings
- Articles
- Notes

Sort them regularly - **BASH** them
- **B**in it!
- **A**ction it **NOW!**
- **S**end it to someone else to call
- **H**old it in the file for a later sort

Keep the file topped up
- You always need more than you think because of the 'fall-out' rate
- They are the header tank for tomorrow's business pipeline

Use the file to
- Plan new campaigns
- Fill up blank spots in the day

POTENTIAL CUSTOMERS

USING THE PROSPECT LIST

Selecting who to call first

- Companies in the same business as your existing customers

- Companies in the same vicinity as your existing customers

- Companies that are in the same vicinity as your company

- Areas that are known to be expanding and spending money

- Where have your colleagues met with success?

- Who have you 'always meant to call but never have'?

- Big companies that you have always been afraid to call; face the fear and do it anyway - it may be that there are many other salespeople who are also afraid to call them. **Who Dares, WINS!**

66

REDUCING RESISTANCE

SELLING TO DIFFERENT PERSONALITIES

Principles

1 Salespeople have their own personalities

2 Customers have their own personalities

3 People like to buy from people with whom they feel comfortable

4 People feel comfortable with people like themselves

5 Salespeople will be selling to customers whose personalities are different
   from their own

6 In this, there is the potential for mismatch

7 The customer doesn't want to change the way they are to suit the salesperson

8 The salesperson must change and reflect the customer's style

SELLING TO DIFFERENT PERSONALITIES

BASIC PERSONALITY TYPES

Introvert/Logical Rationalist Analytical	**Logical/Factual People**	**Extrovert/Logical** Activist Driver
Use 'Auditory' Language: *Hear, Listen, Describe, Word-for-Word, Explain* They like written, documented communication They look for accuracy and detailed evidence and precision	Use 'Kinaesthetic' Language: *Concrete, Touch, Get hold of, Hold it, Real, Doing, Moving* They like direct verbal communications They look for results, action, what it does, how quickly, how much	
Use 'Emotive' Language: *Feels like, Love it, Close, Personal, Meaning* They like conversations and talks - shared communication They look for how it affects people, who uses it, personal benefits	Use 'Visual' Language: *See, Look, Intends, View it, Imagine, Highlight, Crystal clear* They like discussions and brainstorming - 'shoot the breeze' They look for how new/novel it is, long term implications - why is it?	
Introvert/Emotional Loyalist Amiable	**Emotional/Feeling People**	**Extrovert/Emotional** Visionary Expressive

Introverts · Extroverts

REDUCING RESISTANCE

SELLING TO THE 'DRIVER'

The 'driver' is likely to be direct, to the point, abrupt and want to get to the point without any 'beating about the bush'. If they see the benefit, they will make immediate decisions.

Typical traits		How to win them over	
Desires to be:	In charge	Impress them by:	Getting to the point
Wants you to be:	To the point	Ask questions that:	Are relevant
In a meeting:	Initiates and directs	Support their:	Actions
Irritated by:	Indecision and slowness	Demonstrate your:	Experience
		Make benefits:	Tangible and concrete
Pace/timing:	Decisive and fast	Show commitment by:	Getting things done
Looks for:	Productivity		
Time style:	NOW!	Be impressed by:	Their strength
Decisions are:	Closed/final	Best close:	Direct

Watch for: unnecessary power struggles.

SELLING TO THE 'ANALYTICAL'

The 'analytical' is likely to speak in measured tones and be interested in the detail of things. They may want all arguments proved logically, with figures to back up claims, before deciding.

Typical traits		How to win them over	
Desires to be:	Correct/right	Impress them by:	Thoroughness
Wants you to be:	Precise/accurate	Ask questions that:	Are detailed
In a meeting:	Channels and clarifies	Support their:	Thoughts
Irritated by:	Surprises/ unpredictability	Demonstrate your:	Detailed knowledge
		Make benefits:	Provable
Pace/timing:	Systematic and slow	Show commitment	
Looks for:	Accuracy/detail	by:	Being systematic
Time style:	Scheduling	Be impressed by:	Their status
Decisions are:	Deliberate	Best close:	Detailed summary

Watch for: slavishly following the company policy and rules.

REDUCING RESISTANCE

SELLING TO THE 'AMIABLE'

The 'amiable' is likely to be warm, friendly and helpful. They are concerned about the impact on themselves and others. They may look for help from others before taking a decision.

Typical traits		How to win them over	
Desires to be:	Liked/accepted	Impress them by:	Friendliness
Wants you to be:	Pleasant/friendly	Ask questions that:	Are non-threatening
In a meeting:	Harmonising/helpful	Support their:	Feelings
Irritated by:	Impatience/pushness	Demonstrate your:	Team spirit and warmth
Pace/timing:	Comfortable and slow	Make benefits:	Personal
Looks for:	Attention	Show commitment	
Time style:	Then & when - the past	by:	Working with them
Decisions are:	Considered	Be impressed by:	Their loyalty
		Best close:	Assumptive

Watch for: sentimentality and taking things personally.

SELLING TO THE 'EXPRESSIVE'

The 'expressive' is effusive and talkative, with a constant flow of thoughts and ideas. It can be hard to keep up with them, or get a word in edgeways! They are great 'intenders' and procrastinators so you have to pin them down to a commitment.

Typical traits		How to win them over	
Desires to be:	Admired	Impress them by:	Your flexibility
Wants you to be:	Insightful	Ask questions that:	Are far-reaching in their implications
In a meeting:	Explores and questions	Support their:	Ideas
Irritated by:	Routine/the mundane	Demonstrate your:	Originality and creativity
Pace/timing:	Spontaneous and fast	Make benefits:	Innovative and global
Looks for:	Recognition	Show commitment by:	Feeding fresh ideas
Time style:	Procrastinating	Be impressed by:	Their flexibility
Decisions are:	Spontaneous	Best close:	Direct

Watch for: sudden unstructured changes and straying from the point.

73

REDUCING RESISTANCE

HANDLING CONCERNS

Change your thinking!

Get rid of the word **OBJECTIONS** from the vocabulary!

About the only thing a customer **objects** to is being pestered or pushed. But they do have **resistance** to changing suppliers or products and spending more than they feel they have to.

They have concerns and are hesitant because they are not convinced. These are not objections to be overcome, but genuine matters to be resolved.

Follow the six-step sequence

1   Welcome it
2   Question to understand and classify the concern
3   Agree with the customer
4   Answer or outweigh
5   Check satisfaction
6   Close (again)

REDUCING RESISTANCE

HANDLING CONCERNS

SAMPLE CONVERSATION

C/M   'That's too expensive'

S/P   *'That's a very good point, nobody wants to pay more than they have to but, can I just ask you, in what way do you feel it's too expensive?'*

C/M   'It seems to do more than I need'

S/P   *'So, what you're saying is, you wonder if you could get a more basic model cheaper, is that right?'*

C/M   'Yes, I suppose so'

S/P   *'Well, I understand how you **feel**, many of my customers **felt** the same before they looked at the options but they **found** that the features in our model gave them many options that they hadn't considered before. Of course, our full inclusive training meant that they were able to take advantage of these options from day one'*

C/M   'So you'll train my staff, then?'

S/P   *'When we install the equipment, we always ensure that the staff are familiar with all the facilities, and our telephone help line can answer any day to day queries that arise. That's reassuring, isn't it?'*

C/M   'Yes, it may take us some time to get used to it'

S/P   *'So, would you like it delivered on Monday or Tuesday?'*

(75)

CLASSIFYING THE CONCERN

Answering what is meant, not what is said.

- Misunderstandings   Clear them up

- Conditions   Test with 'if'

- Real   **Price**
  Effort
  Risk
  Competition

- Negotiating tactics   Trade - don't just give
  Know your negotiation limits
  Give increased value added

- Answering what is **said** can still leave a concern; we only handle them effectively
  when we deal with what they **mean**

REDUCING RESISTANCE

COMMON CONCERNS

Have answers to common concerns ready

We are happy with our existing supplier	Loyalty = confidence, so get them just to try you as a secondary supplier Look for weaknesses in the competition's offering
You are dearer than others we have seen	Check you are dealing with like for like Remember that you only have to justify the **difference** in price
We don't know your company	Use third party referrals, copy letters from satisfied users, etc
You are a new/small company	New/small = personal service and keen to please If it is a confidence problem, use third party references
I need to check with someone else	Check that, if it were your contact's decision, they would say 'yes' - then offer to help them with information for the other person, or speak to them direct if possible
I want to think about it	Find out what specifically they are considering

Draw up your own matrix with concerns and answers for your company and products. (77)

ANSWERING QUESTIONS

Questions can arise at any time in a call

Tactics to use:

- Don't answer - ask another question
  - *'Do you offer a discount for whole cases?'*
  - **_'Did you want a whole case?'_**

- Answer - follow it with a question
  - *'How soon can you deliver?'*
  - **_'We deliver in your area on a Tuesday, is that OK?'_**

SAMPLE ANSWERS TO CONCERNS

HIGH PRICES

You are dearer than someone else - but your product is better

Prospect: 'You are more expensive than ABC Ltd'

Salesperson: *'Yes, that's true, but let me ask you this, isn't it true that all companies have a choice to make? They can either provide a service that does as much for their customers, OR they can do just enough to get by. That is a choice that every company has to make, isn't it?'*

Prospect: 'Yes, I suppose it is'

Salesperson: *'Well, what would you like us to do for you; as much as possible or just enough to get by?'*

SAMPLE ANSWERS TO CONCERNS
PRICE

Prospect: 'You are dearer than ABC Ltd'

Salesperson: *'Yes, that's true, but let me ask you this; if they were both the same price, which one would you choose?'*

Prospect: 'Yours, I guess'

Salesperson: *'Why would you choose ours?'*
Now list down all the reasons that the Prospect gives you as to why they would choose your product or service - you can even remind them of unique points about your product/service that they may have forgotten, and get their agreement that it should be included in their list.

Salesperson: *'So, isn't it really worth investing just X pounds extra to get all of those additional facilities/advantages/benefits?'*

SAMPLE ANSWERS TO CONCERNS

PRICE

Prospect: 'I can buy others for £300 cheaper'

Salesperson: *'How long do you expect to keep this equipment?'*
Prospect: 'Three years'

Salesperson: *'So, what we are looking at is just £100 per year difference - which is really less than £2 per week, or only 40p per day. When you think about it, that's only 5p an hour for each hour that you are using it.*
Are you really saying that you can't justify an extra 5p an hour to get (then list all the additional reasons for choosing your product or service)?*

This technique is called 'breaking the price down to the ridiculous' to influence the 'Judgement of Value' balance:

SAMPLE ANSWERS TO CONCERNS
NO TRACK RECORD

Prospect: 'I am happy with my existing suppliers'

Salesperson: *'I'm very pleased to hear that, but let me ask you; supposing that, through no fault of their own, your existing supplier was unable to meet an urgent requirement of yours - what would you have to do then?'*

Prospect: 'I'd have to find another supplier'

Salesperson: *'Yes, you would, and would you agree that finding a new supplier in an emergency could mean that you have difficulties with price, quality, opening a new account and so on?'*

Prospect: 'Yes, I suppose it's a possibility'

Salesperson: *'That's why most companies these days have reserve suppliers in place to cater for such emergencies. If you were to order just a small amount from us, you could get to know us and our quality and also open a line of credit, so that if the unforeseen did occur you would already be prepared'*
'Which of our products would you like to try first?'

SAMPLE ANSWERS TO CONCERNS
NO TRACK RECORD

Prospect:	'We've not dealt with you before, how do I know you will do what you say?'
Salesperson:	*'I can appreciate that. Are you saying that, if you were happy that we could do what we say, you'd be prepared to try us?'* (Test close)
Prospect:	'I think so'
Salesperson:	*'If you had a number of our customers there with you today who were happy with our service, would you be guided by what they had to say on our behalf?'*
Prospect:	'Yes'
Salesperson:	Either: *'Well, I have some letters here from our satisfied customers - this is what they have written ...'* (now read the letters - or fax to the prospect) Or: *'Well, I have a list of some of our customers who are happy to talk with you - if I fax you the list, how soon will you be able to speak to them?'* (This is where three-way calling can be a great boon as you can get them on the line immediately)

SAMPLE ANSWERS TO CONCERNS

DELAYING

This often hides a real reason for not proceeding - you need to find out what that is.

Prospect: 'I need some time to consider it'

Salesperson: *'I agree, it is an important decision, isn't it?'* [Prospect agrees]

Salesperson: *'However, in my experience, when someone says to me that they need time to consider it, it is usually because they still have one or two unanswered queries at the back of their minds. Is that a fair comment?'*

Prospect: 'I suppose so'

Salesperson: *'So while we are still on the phone, why don't we make a list of those points so we can see where we are? What are you still unsure about?'*

Listen to each point that is raised, repeat it and summarise briefly, writing it down. They may come up with two or three, rarely more than four.

Salesperson: (reads back list) *'So, if you could satisfy yourself on each of these points, would you be in a position to go ahead?'* [Prospect agrees]
Now answer or outweigh each point, gaining agreement, and close again.

SAMPLE ANSWERS TO CONCERNS

JUST SUPPOSE

Use the power of the imagination - 'Just supposing' 'Imagine'

Prospect: 'I am happy with my current suppliers'

Salesperson: *'Well, just supposing you were convinced that there was another supplier that could offer better products more cost effectively, what would you do?'*

Prospect: 'I am happy with the products we have'

Salesperson: *'Just supposing that you did find a product that was better than the one you were currently using, what would you do?'*

Prospect: 'It is more than I have in budget'

Salesperson: *'Just supposing that you were able to show that the product would save much more than you had allocated in budget, would the board approve an increase?'*

(85)

FINAL TIPS FOR SUCCESS

Perseverance pays!

Remember: Winners never quit and quitters never win!

Regular calling on a company with seemingly little result can put you in the position where you catch them at the right time to win business that salespeople with less perseverance would miss.

Ask for referrals
When you've taken an order from one person/company and they are happy with your service - ask for referrals to others.

> *'Who else is there in your company that I could speak to about our services?'*

Be different!
It is easy to get the same results as others - just do the same things! To get more, we have to be more, do more and do it differently.

Being goal focused, organised, enthusiastic and persistent could just be enough to give you the edge in every sale.   **DO IT NOW!**

TIPS FOR MANAGING THE TELESALES TEAM

TIPS FOR MANAGING THE TELESALES TEAM

THREE TYPES OF MANAGER

What type are you?

1   Those who make things happen
    - **proactive** managers

2   Those who wait for things to happen
    - **reactive** managers

3   Those who wonder what happened
    - **inactive** managers

TIPS FOR MANAGING THE TELESALES TEAM

THREE TYPES OF MANAGER

We can ignore type three! Let's compare the other two types:

Key areas:	Proactive management approach	Reactive management approach
Targets:	Sets achievable targets	Wants 'as much as possible'
Daily activity:	Knows exactly what should happen	Looks to see what people are doing
Monitoring:	Has clear, visible boards on display	Asks (or doesn't)
Competitions:	Has regular, stimulating competitions	Sometimes offers a bottle of wine
Reports:	Asks for simple, quantitative reports	Either complicated, verbose - or none
Training:	Has a plan for regular skills, knowledge and motivational training	Occasionally remembers to give a product quiz
Motivation:	Consistently motivated and inspirational	Goes up and down with the weather!
Sales meetings:	Has regular, relevant sales meetings	Holds a monthly meeting - provided nothing else crops up
Praise:	Regularly catches people doing things right and praises them	Seagull approach - flies round noisily looking for a head to plop on!
Information flow:	Open and willing to share information	Mushroom style - keeps people in the dark and feeds bulls**t
Recognition:	Enjoys recognising success in the team	Begrudges anyone doing well

TIPS FOR MANAGING THE TELESALES TEAM

WHAT DOES YOUR TEAM WANT?

There are 5 universally recognised needs of every employee - identified by John Humble, one of the pioneers of 'Management by Objectives'.

1   Tell me what you expect of me
2   Give me the opportunity to perform
3   Give me guidance when I need it
4   Let me know how I am getting on
5   Reward me according to my contribution

TIPS FOR MANAGING THE TELESALES TEAM

WHAT DOES YOUR TEAM WANT?

Tell me what you expect of me

There are 5 key areas that need to be made clear.

1   The purpose of the job, eg:
    'The telephone salesperson's role is to sell the company's range of products within
    our defined market place to both existing and new customers. The salesperson is
    responsible for achieving profitable, on-target performance in their area.'

2   The **key result areas**, eg: Sales to existing customers by value
                                    Number of new accounts opened
                                    Sales of support agreements, etc

3   The key tasks, eg: Number of contacts per day
                          Number of quotations issued
                          Number of cold calls made

4   The present results for each key task/result area - what has been achieved in
    each of 2 and 3 above?

5   The standard of performance needed for the next period - what are the targets?

(91)

WHAT DOES YOUR TEAM WANT?

Give me the opportunity to perform

'The best executive is the one who has sense enough to pick good people to do what he wants done and enough restraint to keep from meddling with them whilst they are doing it'
- Theodore Roosevelt.

Salespeople need coaching not crushing

- Catch them doing things right - or nearly right
- Praise them for doing well
- Encourage them to keep going when things are tough
- Give them freedom to get it wrong without fear of retribution
- Give special tasks to experienced people to develop them
- Always delegate to develop strengths not to expose weaknesses
- Let them know when you're available to help - and when you are not!

Practise hands-off management as much as possible and hands-on management as much as necessary *'The one-minute manager'*

TIPS FOR MANAGING THE TELESALES TEAM

WHAT DOES YOUR TEAM WANT?

Give me guidance when I need it

- Hold regular meetings to discuss progress
- Correct early before things go too far off-track
- Coach both one-to-one and in groups
- Encourage them to find their own answers to problems
- Guide by questioning: 'Socratic' not 'Didactic'
- Encourage feedback at all times
- Reset goals or reprimand?
  Reset and coach when they **can't** do something
  Reprimand and correct when they **won't** do something

WHAT DOES YOUR TEAM WANT?

Let me know how I am getting on

If an athlete ran a race, and there were no other competitors and no timing, they would have no way of knowing how they got on. In sales it is the same - salespeople have to know how they are doing - they may not keep records themselves, and orders may come in without them knowing.

- Have a computer terminal in the office just for displaying the results so far
- Put up visual, graphic display boards
- Issue regular performance updates
- How are they doing against target?
- How are they doing in comparison with the rest of the team?
- How are they doing in the race to win a competition?

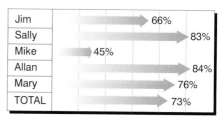

Jim	66%
Sally	83%
Mike	45%
Allan	84%
Mary	76%
TOTAL	73%

Note: Using percentages, rather than actual values, means that those with smaller targets have an equal chance of being up with the leaders.

94

TIPS FOR MANAGING THE TELESALES TEAM

WHAT DOES YOUR TEAM WANT?

Reward me according to my contribution

- Extra commission
- Bonuses
- Profit share
- Special prizes
- Recognition
- Special projects - favourite work
- Time off
- Share in the business
- Personal growth - training
- Freedom
- Bigger desk/chair/office
- Team trips
- Special company events, dinners, etc
- Promotion

SUCCESSFUL SALESPEOPLE

PERSONAL MOTIVATION

**A survey of top producing
salespeople showed:**

93% of the **reasons why they were successful**
were down to personal motivation -

Only 7% was what they knew and their levels of skill

KNOWLEDGE

SKILL

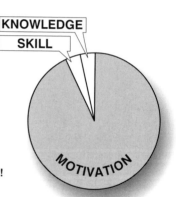

MOTIVATION

**This may make it seem as though knowledge and
skill are not important - this is clearly not the case!
They are VITAL - but ...**

TIPS FOR MANAGING THE TELESALES TEAM

SUCCESSFUL SALESPEOPLE

Knowledge & Skill are the 'payload'

- There is only so much knowledge that a salesperson can have about their company, product or service; imagine that they know all there is to know

- There are only so many skills - how to handle the various stages of a sale; imagine that they know all there is to know

MOTIVATION is like the rocket that lifts the payload.

The bigger the rocket
   - the greater the lift
The bigger the motivation
   - the greater the results

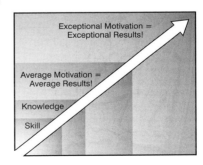

SUCCESSFUL SALESPEOPLE

THE **DAC** FACTOR

There are three key elements to personal motivation

1. Drive
- What makes them 'get up and go' every morning?
- Focus on goals and personal achievement
- Ambition to succeed

2. Attitude
- Positive expectancy
- Willingness to learn and accept assistance
- Always looking for more effective ways to achieve

3. Confidence
- Will perform well - even under pressure
- Believe in the value of the company, product/service
- Can face fresh challenges knowing they can win

TIPS FOR MANAGING THE TELESALES TEAM

SUCCESSFUL SALESPEOPLE

Attributes of top salespeople

Managers have listed the following as being attributes of their top people:

Honesty	Common sense	Humility
Enthusiasm	Knowledge	Strength of character
Positive attitude	Hard working	Dedicated
Confidence	Self respect	Organised
Patience	Caring	Dependable
Discipline	Sense of humour	Decisive
Persistence	Friendly	Listener
Loyalty	Motivated	Communicator
Faith	Compassionate	Learner
Goal oriented	Integrity	Empathetic

Notice how many of these are to do with **D**rive, **A**ttitude and **C**onfidence.

PUTTING BACK THE FUN

To get unusual results, you sometimes have to use unusual methods.

'If you keep on doing what you've always done, you'll keep on getting what you've always got'.

1   Get rid of the chairs. Have everyone standing up for a day and watch the energy!

2   Ring a bell. Whenever someone makes a sale/appointment they run to the front and ring the bell.

3   Bang-Bang! Fill a big net with balloons - one for every sale that is needed in a day. Give each person a pin and they burst one balloon for every sale that they make. Have a prize for the first balloon burst/last one out.

PUTTING BACK THE FUN

4 Bang-Bang-Surprise! As Bang-Bang, but in some of the balloons put additional prizes ; £10 notes, theatre tickets, voucher, etc.

5 Get a supplier to sponsor a 'spiff' day with prizes for selling that supplier's products.

6 Ask the sales team to produce a list of their 'top 20 most impossible prospects to sell to', then get them to swap them with another salesperson. Give prizes for the people who generate most from these 'impossible' files.

TIPS FOR MANAGING THE TELESALES TEAM

ON-GOING TRAINING

1   Purchase a telephone training kit that allows you to record calls; use these for coaching.

2   Give your people regular refreshers through seminars and courses.

3   Include elements of training in the sales meetings.

4   Invite special 'guests' to speak at the meetings.

5   Get your top-producing salespeople involved in training.

6   Build up a library of books, audio and video tapes for training.

7   Always have a budget for training.

8   Invest in your own training.

TIPS FOR MANAGING THE TELESALES TEAM

FINALLY ...

'You never work for sombody else. Someone else might sign the cheque but you're the one who fills in the amount'

'Of all the things you wear, your expression is the most important'
– Janet Lane

'When you're looking at the sun, you see no shadows'
– Helen Keller

'Obstacles are what you see when you take your eyes off your goals'

'It's your **attitude** not your **aptitude** that determines your **altitude**'

'Those who say it can't be done are usually interrupted by others doing it'

'The difference between ordinary and extraordinary is that little extra'

'Success is simply a matter of luck. Ask any failure'

Where eagles dare!

In each age, men of genius undertake the ascent.
From below, the world follows them with their eyes.
These men go up the mountain, enter the clouds,
disappear, reappear. People watch them and mark them.

They walk by the side of precipices. They daringly pursue their road.
See them aloft, see them in the distance; they are but black specks. On they go.
The road is uneven, its difficulties constant. At each step a wall, at each step a trap.

As they rise the cold increases. They must make their ladder, cut the ice and walk on it,
hewing the steps in haste. A storm is raging. Nevertheless, they go forward in their
madness. The air becomes difficult to breathe. The abyss yawns below them.
Some fall. Others stop and retrace their steps; there is sad weariness.

The bold ones continue. They are eyed by the eagles; the lightning plays about them;
the hurricane is furious. No matter, they persevere.

Victor Hugo

When God made the oyster, He guaranteed him absolute economical and social security. He built the oyster a house, a shell, to protect him from his enemies.

When hungry, the oyster simply opens his shell and food rushes in for him. He has no worries, he doesn't fight anybody. He's not going anywhere.

But, when God made the eagle, He gave him the sky as his domain. The eagle then nested on the highest crag, where the storms threaten every day. For food, he flies through miles of rain, snow, sleet and wind. He screams his defiance at the elements and goes about his own business building his life. When aroused, he's a vicious foe for his enemies.

The eagle, not the oyster, is the symbol of achievement.

THE MANAGEMENT POCKETBOOK SERIES

Pocketbooks

Appraisals
Assertiveness
Balance Sheet
Business Planning
Business Writing
Call Centre Customer Care
Career Transition
Challengers
Coaching
Communicator's
Competencies
Controlling Absenteeism
Creative Manager's
C.R.M.
Cross-cultural Business
Cultural Gaffes
Customer Service
Decision-making
Developing People
Discipline
Diversity
E-commerce
Emotional Intelligence
Employment Law
Empowerment

Energy and Well-being
Facilitator's
Flexible Workplace
Handling Complaints
Icebreakers
Impact & Presence
Improving Efficiency
Improving Profitability
Induction
Influencing
International Trade
Interviewer's
I.T. Trainer's
Key Account Manager's
Leadership
Learner's
Manager's
Managing Budgets
Managing Cashflow
Managing Change
Managing Recruitment
Managing Upwards
Managing Your Appraisal
Marketing
Meetings

Mentoring
Motivation
Negotiator's
Networking
NLP
Openers & Closers
People Manager's
Performance Management
Personal Success
Positive Mental Attitude
Presentations
Problem Behaviour
Problem Solving
Project Management
Quality
Resolving Conflict
Sales Excellence
Salesperson's
Self-managed Development
Starting In Management
Strategy
Stress
Succeeding at Interviews
Teambuilding Activities
Teamworking

Telephone Skills
Telesales
Thinker's
Time Management
Trainer Standards
Trainer's
Training Evaluation
Training Needs Analysis
Virtual Teams
Vocal Skills

Pocketsquares

Great Training Robbery
Hook Your Audience

Pocketfiles

Trainer's Blue Pocketfile of
Ready-to-use Activities

Trainer's Green Pocketfile of
Ready-to-use Activities

Trainer's Red Pocketfile of
Ready-to-use Activities

27.2.06

About the Author

Peter Wyllie
Peter spent over 30 years in sales, sales management and training. In recent years he has, in his own words, 'gone into semi-retirement'.

Peter works in interim management for a variety of companies. He is regularly a compere for charity events and an after dinner speaker.

He writes speciality humorous odes for both business and social occasions via his website www.proverse.co.uk and his personal website www.peter-wyllie.com.

Contact
Peter's email address is peter.wyllie@tiscali.co.uk

ORDER FORM

Your details

Name _____

Position _____

Company _____

Address _____

_____

_____

Telephone _____

Fax _____

E-mail _____

VAT No. (EC companies) _____

Your Order Ref _____

Please send me:

	No. copies
The Telesales Pocketbook	
The _____ Pocketbook	
The _____ Pocketbook	
The _____ Pocketbook	
The _____ Pocketbook	

Order by Post

MANAGEMENT POCKETBOOKS LTD

LAUREL HOUSE, STATION APPROACH,
ALRESFORD, HAMPSHIRE SO24 9JH UK

Order by Phone, Fax or Internet

Telephone: +44 (0)1962 735573
Facsimile: +44 (0)1962 733637
E-mail: sales@pocketbook.co.uk
Web: www.pocketbook.co.uk

MANAGEMENT POCKETBOOKS